PICKLEBALL

by Martha London

The Greater World of Sports

SportsZone

An Imprint of Abdo Publishing | abdobooks.com

abdobooks.com

Published by Abdo Publishing, a division of ABDO, PO Box 398166, Minneapolis, Minnesota 55439.

Printed in the United States of America, North Mankato, Minnesota
092019
012020

THIS BOOK CONTAINS RECYCLED MATERIALS

Cover Photo: Deerfield Photo/Shutterstock Images
Interior Photos: David Brewster/Star Tribune/Getty Images, 4–5; Bill Oxford/iStockphoto, 6, 17; Rich Legg/iStockphoto, 8, 11, 22; Arne Beruldsen/Shutterstock Images, 12; Jeff Gritchen/MediaNews Group/Orange County Register/Getty Images, 14–15; iStockphoto, 19; Ron Alvey/Shutterstock Images, 20; Dennis MacDonald/Alamy, 24–25; BH Pix/iStockphoto, 26, 28

Editor: Melissa York
Series Designer: Melissa Martin

Library of Congress Control Number: 2019941977

Publisher's Cataloging-in-Publication Data

Names: London, Martha, author
Title: Pickleball / by Martha London
Description: Minneapolis, Minnesota : Abdo Publishing, 2020 | Series: The greater world of sports | Includes online resources and index
Identifiers: ISBN 9781532190407 (lib. bdg.) | ISBN 9781532176258 (ebook)
Subjects: LCSH: Pickleball (Game)--Juvenile literature. | Racket games--Juvenile literature. | Recreations--Juvenile literature. | Sports--Juvenile literature.
Classification: DDC 796.34--dc23

TABLE OF CONTENTS

Chapter 1

A GAME FOR EVERYONE

A group of adult volunteers gathered on an outdoor court. A youth group was learning to play pickleball. Twenty boys and girls from the group surrounded the volunteers. The sun shone on the warm summer day. White lines marked the courts. Nets divided the courts into two sides.

It wasn't tennis. It wasn't badminton, either. This afternoon, the kids were learning how to play pickleball. And the volunteers were ready to teach them.

Pickleball is a great sport for kids and adults to play together.

PICKLEBALL
Bonita Springs Fl.
PICKLEBALL

Each volunteer gathered with a small group of kids to show them the basics. The kids held the paddles in their hands. They bounced the small ball around. It looked like a wiffle ball. Soon sets of four players were volleying back and forth. The volunteers watched and refereed the games.

The pickleball court and net look similar to a tennis court and net, but there are key differences.

Yellow and orange balls flew everywhere around the court. Kids and adults laughed. The volunteers explained to the kids that pickleball is about precision. One woman told her young partner that the key to the game is "putting the ball where the other person isn't."

By the end of the afternoon, many of the kids got the hang of the game. A few even had rallies.

A Growing Sport

Kids all over the United States are learning pickleball. The Boys and Girls Club, a youth group, said that between November 2018 and March 2019, approximately 800 kids from Massachusetts alone had started pickleball lessons. The program averaged about 20 kids per day.

Boys and Girls Club participants said their program was a success. Part of its success was due to the connection between adult volunteers

and kids. Pickleball is a great sport that keeps people active. But it's also a great sport for building community.

Pickleball is a newer sport compared to other popular activities. It was designed to be played by multiple generations at the same time. The court is small, and the paddles are lightweight. Games can be as easy-going or competitive as the players want. The most important part of pickleball is having fun.

People with different levels of physical ability can play pickleball.

Chapter 2

THE HISTORY OF PICKLEBALL

Three men from Bainbridge Island, Washington, created pickleball in 1965. One Saturday, Joel Pritchard and Bill Bell went to an old badminton court in Pritchard's backyard. They wanted a game that everyone in their families could play. They used Ping-Pong paddles and a wiffle ball. Their families played all weekend. A week later Pritchard and Bell brought in their friend, Barney McCallum. Together, the three men started creating more rules for this new game.

Making a New Game

At first, the net reached the usual badminton height of 60 inches (1.5 m). The court was made

Pickleball has always been a sport for players young and old.

The pickleball net is low to the ground.

of asphalt. When the ball hit the ground, it bounced. This gave the men an idea. They lowered the net. Now it was 36 inches (0.9 m) high.

The men and their families, including their kids, played the game. They tried out different rules. Over time, the game of pickleball was created.

Pickleball spread throughout the area. In 1967 the first dedicated pickleball court was built in Pritchard's neighborhood. Other courts popped up on tennis courts and in driveways where people drew the lines in chalk.

Growing Quickly

As of 2018, the Sport and Fitness Industry Association (SFIA) estimated that there were more than 3.1 million pickleball players in the United States alone. SFIA expects that number to continue to rise as school and community education organizations create more pickleball programs.

Nine years later, the first pickleball tournament was held. Many of the participants were college tennis players. They didn't know a lot about pickleball. But they were excited to learn.

Picking Up Steam

News about pickleball spread with help from *Tennis* magazine and other publications. It was soon time to create an organization that would

ENGAGE
Pickleball
ENGAGE
Pickleball

oversee the sport. The USA Pickleball Association (USAPA) was founded in 1984. The USAPA created a rule book to help standardize play. The USAPA advertised tournaments and sponsored new courts to help the new sport grow. Having a standard rule book would let people from across the United States all use the same rules. This way they could play pickleball together.

Today, people from all 50 states play pickleball. More courts are being built, often connected to senior-living buildings. Pritchard, Bell, and McCallum wanted a game that every person could play and enjoy. From young kids to senior citizens, pickleball is open to everyone.

Many pickleball groups hold tournaments.

Chapter 3

RULES OF THE GAME

Some aspects of pickleball are similar to tennis, Ping-Pong or table tennis, and other racket sports. But there are a few rules and pieces of equipment that are specific to pickleball.

Equipment

Pickleball players use paddles instead of rackets. The paddles are bigger than those used in table tennis. Sometimes they are round and sometimes they are shaped like a rectangle. Originally the paddles were made out of wood. Paddles today are usually made of a light composite material. Now they are lighter, but they still have

Pickleball is played with a large paddle and a lightweight plastic ball with holes.

a hard face. The paddles don’t have a rubber coating like table-tennis paddles.

The ball resembles a wiffle ball. It is not the small, hollow ball of Ping-Pong or the soft felted rubber of tennis. Pickleballs and official wiffle balls both have holes and are made of plastic. Pickleballs have different holes than wiffle balls and are slightly larger. The ball is often yellow in color.

The court looks a lot like a tennis court, but it is the size of a badminton court. Like tennis, there are right and left areas on each side of the net where players serve the ball, and the net is low to the ground. Unlike tennis, the pickleball court is the same size whether two people or four people are playing.

PICKLEBALL COURT

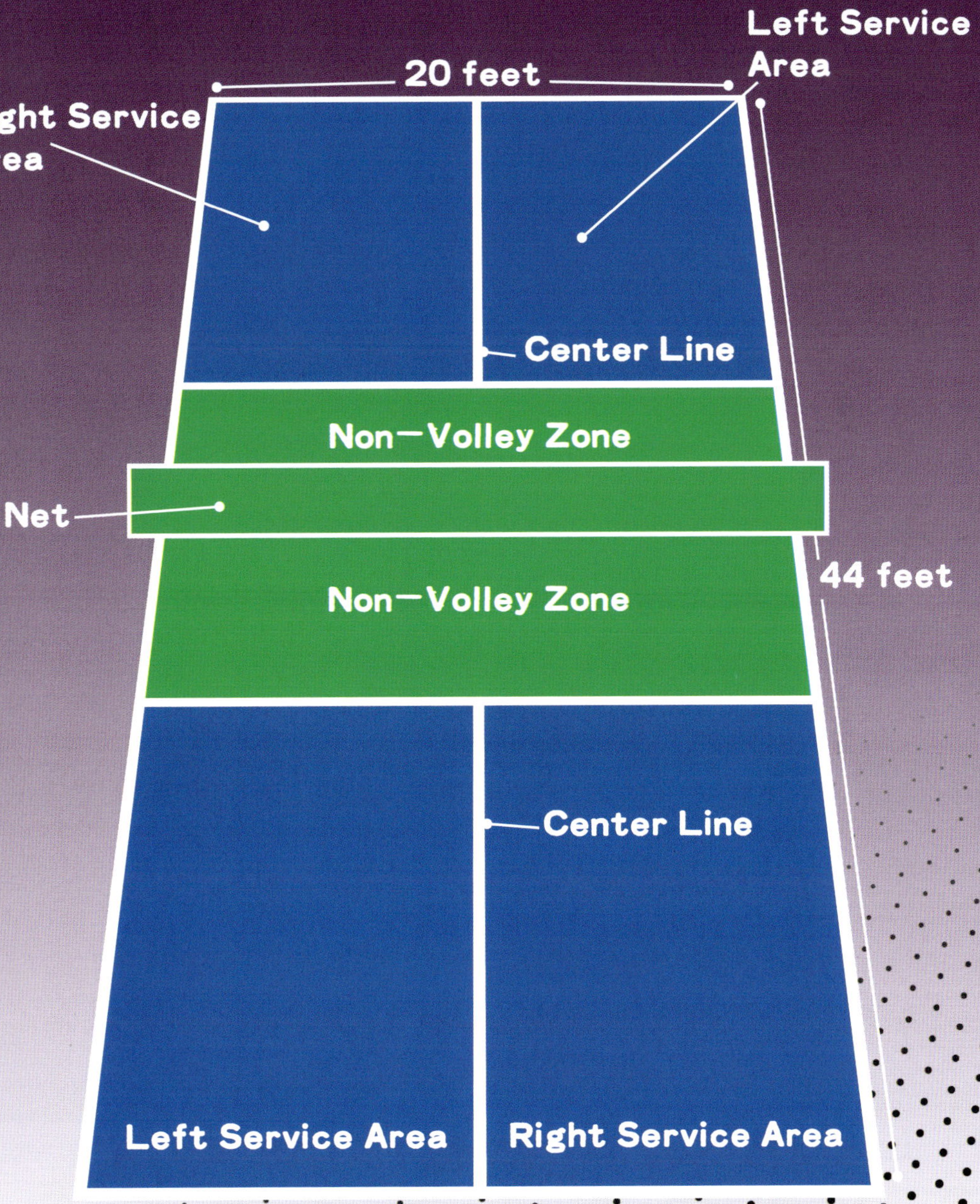

Rules about serving keep pickleball a sport of precision over strength.

Rules of Play

Pickleball matches are usually played in the best two-out-of-three games fashion. Each game is played until a player or doubles team has 11 points. The winning player or team must win by two points. Unlike many other racket sports, only the side serving the ball can win a point. If the receiving team wins the point, they begin serving. Now they have a chance to score points. The serving team continues to serve until they make a fault. A fault is when a point ends. That could be because of a missed serve, hitting a ball out of bounds, or being unable to return a ball in the rally.

Players have to serve in a particular way. They cannot serve overhand as in tennis. Players must serve underhand. The wrist and paddle need to stay below the player's waist. Instead of relying on speed, pickleball serves need to be accurate and push opponents away from the net. To keep opponents back, good servers often lob the ball deep into the service area.

Pickleball also has a double-bounce rule and a non-volley area. The double-bounce rule means

Players must be back from the net outside the non-volley zone to hit the ball without it bouncing first.

that after the serve, both sides must let the ball bounce before hitting it. Players cannot volley until the ball has bounced on their side of the net. This is required with every serve before a volley can start.

The non-volley area is the first seven feet on either side of the net. It also includes the white lines that outline the area. Players are not allowed to step into the non-volley area, not even on the lines, to volley the ball. They can volley outside of the area. But if the player steps in the non-volley area, the player must let the ball bounce. If a player steps into the non-volley area and volleys, that is a fault, and the point is over.

To volley, the player must have both feet outside of the non-volley area. The double-bounce rule and non-volley zone allow pickleball to be a game about finesse, accuracy, and strategy, rather than a competition to see who can hit the ball hardest.

The Court and the Kitchen

The non-volley zone is also called the kitchen. People aren't sure where the term came from, but one theory is that it was borrowed from the game shuffleboard. A disc landing in the 10 Off area, also called the kitchen, results in a loss of 10 points in shuffleboard. In pickleball, volleying in the kitchen results in a fault and the end of the rally.

Chapter 4

PICKLEBALL TOURNAMENTS

After the first tournament was held in Washington in 1976, other pickleball tournaments began popping up. At first, most of the large tournaments were for seniors. One of the largest of these is part of the National Senior Games.

The National Senior Games (NSG) is held around the United States every other year. In 2019, it was held in Albuquerque, New Mexico. It had almost 14,000 participants in 20 different sports. One of those sports was pickleball. More than 1,100 seniors played pickleball at the NSG.

Seniors compete in tournaments around the country to qualify for the National Senior Games every other year.

Citrus Hills

Pickleball is often associated with older players. Seventy-five percent of pickleball players who play eight or more times a year are over the age of 55. Many senior citizens play pickleball to

Good sportsmanship is an important part of pickleball.

stay active. Some older pickleball players enjoyed other racket sports such as tennis when they were younger. But the quick movement needed to play those games makes participating more difficult for seniors. Pickleball is more accessible.

But seniors aren't the only people playing pickleball. The sport is spreading across the United States and the world. Tournaments are available for players of all ages now, but players don't have to wait for a tournament to play. Many pickleball players prefer to play for fun at local courts.

Etiquette

Pickleball is a fun, fast-paced sport, so players sometimes get pretty excited. The sound of quick volleys and excited shouts from players means the game can be loud. Part of the etiquette of playing pickleball isn't just how to treat opponents.

Players also have to be respectful of people who aren't playing.

Some pickleball courts are surrounded by homes in the middle of a neighborhood. Players encourage each other to be respectful of the people in the community by not playing after dark or too early in the morning. If a neighbor does come to the court to ask players to be quieter, it is the players' responsibility to respect that request. They don't have to stop playing. But it's important to recognize that the sport affects others too. When players are respectful, pickleball is a great sport that can bring together people of all ages.

Pickleball is growing. It's becoming easier to find courts and friends to join the fun. It's a great way to exercise and meet new friends. Because of the mix of intense rallies and a small court, pickleball is becoming the perfect sport for many people.

Pickleball is great for making new friends and having fun.

GLOSSARY

accessible

Easy to use.

asphalt

A hard surface to walk or play games on.

competitive

A situation where multiple people want to win.

composite

Made of multiple materials.

etiquette

The proper behavior for the game.

fault

A mistake a player makes that ends the rally.

finesse

Skillful play.

lob

A high, looping shot.

precision

Being exact and accurate.

rally

A series of shots back and forth across the net.

referee

A sports official who keeps score or makes sure players follow the rules.

serve

Beginning the point in pickleball by hitting the ball first.

volley

Hitting the ball with the paddle before it hits the ground.

MORE INFORMATION

BOOKS

Decker, Michael. *Dodgeball*. Minneapolis, MN: Abdo Publishing, 2020.

Littlewood, Mary. *Pickleball Fundamentals*. Champaign, IL: Human Kinetics, 2015.

Marthaler, Jon. *Offbeat Sports*. Minneapolis, MN: Abdo Publishing, 2018.

ONLINE RESOURCES

Booklinks
NONFICTION NETWORK
FREE! ONLINE NONFICTION RESOURCES

To learn more about pickleball, please visit **abdobooklinks.com** or scan this QR code. These links are routinely monitored and updated to provide the most current information available.

INDEX

ABOUT THE AUTHOR

Martha London writes books for young readers full time. When she isn't writing, you can find her hiking in the woods.